LEADERSHIP
Is an
ART

"Astonishing."
—President Bill Clinton

Also by Max De Pree:

LEADERSHIP JAZZ

—————— Max De Pree ——————

LEADERSHIP
Is an
ART

A DELL TRADE PAPERBACK

A DELL TRADE PAPERBACK
Published by
Dell Publishing
a division of
Bantam Doubleday Dell Publishing Group, Inc.
1540 Broadway, New York, New York 10036

The trademark Dell® is registered in the U.S. Patent and Trademark Office.

ISBN: 0-440-50324-8

Reprinted by arrangement with Doubleday
Printed in the United States of America
Published simultaneously in Canada
September 1990

20 19 18 17 16

BVG

To mine from yours

ACKNOWLEDGMENTS

Editor
Clark Malcolm

True Critics
Jody Handy
Lewis Smedes
Patrick Thompson

Contributors
All the folks at Herman Miller and elsewhere
who taught me—and are teaching me—
the art of leadership.

CONTENTS

CONTENTS

FOREWORD:
HISTORY, LEADERSHIP,
AND A VISION FOR
CORPORATE LIFE

I wish I could claim to have been the first to notice that Herman Miller, Inc. is a brilliantly managed company. But, in truth, the secret has been out for a long time. The company was founded in 1923 by D. J. De Pree, and it has generated ripples of distinction—and waves of innovation—since the 1930s.

Since finishing this marvelous book by Max De Pree (D.J.'s son and the current chief executive officer of Herman Miller), I've been racking my brain trying to remember when I initially became aware of the existence of the company. It occurs to me that I may have slipped into my first Eames chair in the early 1950s; nonetheless, being that I was no more than seven or eight at the time, I doubt I was told that the masterpiece of comfort and elegant design in which I was so contentedly ensconced was manufactured by a company named Herman Miller. (And, not until considerably later would I learn that original Eames chairs were in the permanent collections of New York's Museum of Modern Art and the Louvre's Musée des Arts Décoratifs.)

But moving forward through my memory some thirty years, I know I was familiar enough with Herman Miller not to be surprised when, in 1983, it was chosen by Milton Moskowitz and his colleagues as one of "the 100 Best Companies to Work for in America." It seemed an obvious choice to me at the time. Ah, and now I remember why! I *first* heard of Herman Miller in 1972. That's the year when America woke to the Japanese industrial challenge, and hundreds of management consultants like me were sent scurrying about trying to find ways to improve U.S. manufacturing productivity. That was the year I "discovered" the Scanlon Plan, that "effective and humane" method by which workers are motivated to find ways to improve the quantity and quality of their work.

The Scanlon idea is simple: When workers suggest ways to improve productivity they are cut into the financial gains that result from their contributions. When I learned about the Scanlon Plan, I thought it was a brilliant idea—and I still do. But, ho-hum, I discovered that, in 1972, the Scanlon Plan had already been the modus operandi at Herman Miller for some *twenty* years!

In fact, since then I've learned that nearly every mark of managerial eminence that I could subsequently "discover" could be found routinely in operation at the Herman Miller company. That's why a lot of people like me —professors of management, business journalists, and management consultants—spend seemingly inordinate amounts of time studying the Herman Miller system and following the company's remarkable progress. And there are scores of reasons to track Herman Miller's impressive performance. Here's a sample:

First, it's an extremely profitable business: A hundred dollars invested in Herman Miller stock in 1975 had grown in value to—and let me be exact about this—$4,854.60 in 1986 (to save you getting out your calculator, that's a compounded annual rate of growth of 41 percent). Among the *Fortune* 500, "little" Herman Miller may only be ranked 456th in total sales, but it is ranked seventh in terms of total return to investors over ten years. (That's what financial people call the bottom line.)

Second, other furniture companies have more employees, but the Herman Miller folks are the industry's most productive (measured in terms of net income per employee). And, while some of their competitors may be bigger on this measure or that, Herman Miller outspends them all nearly two to one, on average, on design and

R&D. (Productive Workers + Innovative Products = Industry Leadership, no?)

Third, who could overlook the company's innovativeness? I have already mentioned all that money Herman Miller spends on R&D and design. But what is even more impressive than their expenditures is their results: The open office, the wall-attached desk, stackable chairs, "Ethospace Interiors" (if that's an unfamiliar term, just imagine "translucence and modularity" and you're on your way)—these, and many more, are all Herman Miller innovations. How, you might ask, could such radical design ideas come from a company headquartered in Zeeland, Michigan, a frosty town with no bars, no pool halls, and no theaters? Don't all top designers live in New York, Paris, or Rome? They all came to Zeeland, Max says, because D. J. De Pree and Max's brother Hugh, who preceded Max as President, "had the strength to abandon themselves to the wild ideas of others." D.J. talked many of the greatest designers of the century—Gilbert Rhode, Charles Eames, and Robert Propst—into visiting Zeeland, where he promised them a free hand in designing what Eames calls "good goods." D.J. and, later, Hugh promised them that they would keep pesky executives, salespeople, and engineers from "making a little change here and there" in their designs. You see, D.J. had decided that there was a market for good design and that great designers needed freedom to try out their wild ideas. In short, D.J. concluded a long time ago that Herman Miller would be a leader, not a follower. And it still is.

Fourth, Max, like his dad, believes in the rule of "abandoning oneself to the strengths of others." Not just "expert" others—that is, not just world-class designers and people with university degrees, but (trusting the strengths of) all Herman Miller employees. For example, through the Scanlon Plan, workers make suggestions to management for ways to improve such things as customer service, quality, and productivity. In 1987–88, Herman Miller employees made suggestions that led to cost savings of some twelve million dollars (or, about three thousand dollars for every U.S. employee). In fact, one day a month, top managers report to workers on the company's productivity and profits—the kind of information that is normally hoarded in most big U.S. firms—and the managers also report on the status of all those employee suggestions. Why do the employees care? Because they are owners of the company (100 percent of all regular employees who have worked there for at least a year own company stock, and over 50 percent regularly purchase shares in addition to those that come as a benefit of employment). "Around here," says Max, "the employees act as if they own the place."

And fifth, but most important, Herman Miller is a place with integrity. Max defines integrity as "a fine sense of one's obligations." That integrity exhibits itself in the company's dedication to superior design, to quality, to making a contribution to society—and in its manifest respect for its customers, investors, suppliers, and employees. Integrity comes out in lots of little ways. For example, while executives in other companies were busy "taking care of number one" by arranging Golden Parachutes for themselves, in 1986 Herman Miller introduced Silver Parachutes for all its employees with over two years of service. In case of an unfriendly takeover of Herman Miller that led to termination of employment, the Silver Parachute plan would offer a soft landing for the kind of people in the ranks of the organization whose welfare is ignored in most corporations. But then, Herman Miller isn't like most other business organizations.

Is it any wonder that a 1988 *Fortune* poll picked Herman Miller as one of the nation's "ten most admired companies"? (And not only was it ranked first in its industry, it was fourth out of *all* U.S. companies in the category of "quality of products or services.")

But as impressive as all of this is, none of these distinctions is the main reason why I commend Max's book to all leaders and would-be leaders. No, my enthusiastic endorsement is based on the conviction that this is the best book ever written on the subject of business leadership. Of the dozen or so books published in the last few years that have stressed the role of the leader in achieving corporate excellence, this is the only one that puts forward one forgotten but essential truth about leadership: *Leaders have ideas.* In those other books, leaders are portrayed, variously, as charismatic personalities, showmen, cheerleaders, con artists, visionaries, autocrats, and circus stunt men. They bark orders and run around doing everybody else's work for them. How preposterous that this could work in a company of one thousand (let alone a hundred thousand) employees! Max's idea of leadership is different. He knows from his experience that it is not a leader's strong voice, the snap of his whip, or his trendy TV persona that motivates employees. The art of leadership, as Max says, is "liberating people to do what is required of them in the most effective and humane way possible." Thus, the leader is the "servant" of his followers in that he removes the obstacles that prevent them from doing their jobs. In short, the true leader enables his or her followers to realize their full potential.

To do this effectively requires clear thinking on the part of the leader. That is, leaders must be clear about their own beliefs: They must have thought through their assumptions about human nature, the role of the organization, the measurement of performance (and the host of other issues that are included in several extremely useful lists of Socratic questions that Max peppers throughout the book). Because they will have carefully considered such questions in advance, leaders will have the self-confidence, as Max says, to "encourage contrary opinions" and "to abandon themselves to the strengths of others." In short, the true leader is a *listener.* The leader listens to the ideas, needs, aspirations, and wishes of the followers and then—within the context of his or her own well-developed system of beliefs—responds to these in an appropriate fashion. That is why the leader must know his own mind. That is why leadership requires ideas. And that is what this book is: a compendium of ideas about organizational leadership.

One question remains: Does it work? (Does Max De Pree practice the art of leadership he describes in these pages? Is the obvious success of Herman Miller related to Max's leadership?) The answer is an unqualified yes. Bear in mind that that affirmative comes from a skeptic who has learned (painfully) that there is almost always a gap between what a CEO *claims* his philosophy to be and what he, in fact, does on the job. Hence, for a time, I had treated what Max De Pree says about the art of management as mere theory until I could put it to the ultimate test of asking his followers what *they* thought of Herman Miller's top management. Then I got my first chance to visit a Herman Miller factory. I was given *carte blanche* to go anywhere and talk to anyone, managers and workers. The only problem was that I couldn't tell one from the other! People who seemed to be production workers were engaged in solving the "managerial" problems of improving productivity and quality. People who seemed to be managers had their sleeves rolled up and were working, side by side, with everybody else in an all-out effort to produce the best products in the most effective way. "The signs of outstanding leadership are found among the followers," Max writes in this wonderful little book.

They certainly are. I found that Max's excellence as a

leader was manifested in the productive spirit of *self-management* that I found in every Herman Miller employee—worker or manager—with whom I spoke. Among the dozens of corporations I had previously visited, I'd never seen anything like it. I discovered not only that Max practiced what he preached, but so did the people who worked for him—the people he *served*. These were people who were dedicated to the beliefs and ideas that Max espoused, particularly to the idea that Herman Miller must keep changing and improving its products, and must continually renew its enterprising spirit to remain competitive in the years to come.

Now, that's the kind of company a person would invest in if he had particular reason to care about the future. At least, that's what I did. A while back, I took money I'd been saving for my youngest daughter's college education and invested it in Herman Miller stock. Because I cared about my daughter's future, I wanted to invest in a company that *had* a future. And thanks to the legacy of leadership that Max De Pree will leave behind at Herman Miller, what a glorious future that promises to be!

JAMES O'TOOLE

Graduate School of Business

University of Southern California

INTRODUCTION

You can start this book anywhere. It is more a book of ideas than practices. It is not what most people would describe as a management book on how to get things done—though the beliefs expressed here may help you do some extremely important things. The book is about the art of leadership: liberating people to do what is required of them in the most effective and humane way possible.

It is not a book of facts or history. Though I like to tell stories, the book is not filled with anecdotes. Since it deals more with ideas and beliefs and relationships, it has to do with the "why" of institutional and corporate life rather than the "how." Profit, the hoped-for result of the "how," is normal and essential. Those results, however, are only a way to measure our resourcefulness at a point in time, mile markers on a long road. Why we get those results is more important. That's what this book is about.

A lot of people helped me create this book, some of them unwittingly. A number of them are mentioned by name. There are a good many references to Herman Miller, Inc. This is quite natural because of the forty years I have worked there. You should not be surprised, then, that I have a good opinion of the company. The people there have become my second family. Many of you who read this book may see yourselves in it. Perhaps we have never met, but it is not mysterious to me that this should be so.

In any case, the ideas and beliefs and principles in this book apply to nearly all group activity. Healthy relationships of different kinds can be built in almost any organization.

Charles Eames taught me the usefulness of repetition. I often repeat myself, by design, to establish something and then connect it to something else. A new situation requires another connection because things appear in a new way and need relationships to what I already know.

Leadership is an art, something to be learned over time, not simply by reading books. Leadership is more tribal than scientific, more a weaving of relationships than an amassing of information, and, in that sense, I don't know how to pin it down in every detail.

In some sense, every reader "finishes" every book according to his or her experiences and needs and beliefs and potential. That is the way you can really own a book. Buying books is easy; owning them is not. There is space for you to finish and own this book. The ideas here have been in my mind for quite a few years, changing, growing, maturing. I will continue to work on them long after this book is published, and I trust you will too.

In saying this, I am expressing the hope that you will see that the book demands something of you and that the book is open to your influence and your observations. This book, as you read it, should illustrate many of the ideas discussed, especially ones of participation and ownership. I hope this book, like many well-thought-out buildings, is indeterminate.

As a child, I often watched adults study books and learned one of my first lessons about reading. They wrote in their books. Intent and involved readers often write in the margins and between the lines. (You may end up doing a lot of writing and reading between the lines in this book!) Good readers take possession of what they are learning by underlining and commenting and questioning. In this manner, they "finish" what they read.

You can read this book quickly, but I hope you cannot

finish it quickly. It will be worth a lot more to you if you finish it, if you have made it truly your own book.

Many years ago Herman Miller was building an addition to one of its plants. The steel was up when the job superintendent noticed that something was wrong. He discovered that the addition was eight inches too high. All the columns had to be cut off. I had two of the ends chrome plated. They stand in my office, as a kind of folk sculpture, to remind me that no one is perfect. That goes for books too.

THE
MILLWRIGHT DIED

My father is ninety-six years old. He is the founder of Herman Miller, and much of the value system and impounded energy of the company, a legacy still drawn on today, is a part of his contribution. In the furniture industry of the 1920s the machines of most factories were not run by electric motors, but by pulleys from a central drive shaft. The central drive shaft was run by the steam engine. The steam engine got its steam from the boiler. The boiler, in our case, got its fuel from the sawdust and other waste coming out of the machine room—a beautiful cycle.

The millwright was the person who oversaw that cycle

and on whom the entire activity of the operation depended. He was a key person.

One day the millwright died.

My father, being a young manager at the time, did not particularly know what he should do when a key person died, but thought he ought to go visit the family. He went to the house and was invited to join the family in the living room. There was some awkward conversation—the kind with which many of us are familiar.

The widow asked my father if it would be all right if she read aloud some poetry. Naturally, he agreed. She went into another room, came back with a bound book, and for many minutes read selected pieces of beautiful poetry. When she finished, my father commented on how beautiful the poetry was and asked who wrote it. She replied that her husband, the millwright, was the poet.

It is now nearly sixty years since the millwright died, and my father and many of us at Herman Miller continue to wonder: Was he a poet who did millwright's work, or was he a millwright who wrote poetry?

In our effort to understand corporate life, what is it we should learn from this story? In addition to all of the ratios and goals and parameters and bottom lines, it is fundamental that leaders endorse a concept of persons. This begins with an understanding of the diversity of people's gifts and talents and skills.

Understanding and accepting diversity enables us to see that each of us is needed. It also enables us to begin to think about being abandoned to the strengths of others, of admitting that we cannot *know* or *do* everything.

The simple act of recognizing diversity in corporate life helps us to connect the great variety of gifts that people bring to the work and service of the organization. Diversity allows each of us to contribute in a special way, to make our special gift a part of the corporate effort.

Recognizing diversity helps us to understand the need

we have for opportunity, equity, and identity in the workplace. Recognizing diversity gives us the chance to provide meaning, fulfillment, and purpose, which are not to be relegated solely to private life any more than are such things as love, beauty, and joy. It also helps us to understand that for many of us there is a fundamental difference between goals and rewards.

In the end, diversity is not only real in our corporate groups but, as with the millwright, it frequently goes unrecognized. Or as another poet, Thomas Gray, put it, talent may go unnoticed and unused.

> Full many a gem of purest ray serene,
>   The dark unfathomed caves of ocean bear:
> Full many a flower is born to blush unseen,
>   And waste its sweetness on the desert air.

When we think about leaders and the variety of gifts people bring to corporations and institutions, we see that the art of leadership lies in polishing and liberating and enabling those gifts.

10

WHAT *IS* LEADERSHIP?

The first responsibility of a leader is to define reality. The last is to say thank you. In between the two, the leader must become a servant and a debtor. That sums up the progress of an artful leader.

Concepts of leadership, ideas about leadership, and leadership practices are the subject of much thought, discussion, writing, teaching, and learning. True leaders are sought after and cultivated. Leadership is not an easy subject to explain. A friend of mine characterizes leaders simply like this: "Leaders don't inflict pain; they bear pain."

The goal of thinking hard about leadership is not to

produce great or charismatic or well-known leaders. The measure of leadership is not the quality of the head, but the tone of the body. The signs of outstanding leadership appear primarily among the followers. Are the followers reaching their potential? Are they learning? Serving? Do they achieve the required results? Do they change with grace? Manage conflict?

I would like to ask you to think about the concept of leadership in a certain way. Try to think about a leader, in the words of the gospel writer Luke, as "one who serves." Leadership is a concept of owing certain things to the institution. It is a way of thinking about institutional heirs, a way of thinking about stewardship as contrasted with ownership. Robert Greenleaf has written an excellent book about this idea, *Servant Leadership.*

The art of leadership requires us to think about the leader-as-steward in terms of relationships: of assets and legacy, of momentum and effectiveness, of civility and values.

Leaders should leave behind them assets and a legacy. First, consider assets; certainly leaders owe assets. Leaders owe their institutions vital financial health, and the relationships and reputation that enable continuity of that financial health. Leaders must deliver to their organizations the appropriate services, products, tools, and equipment that people in the organization need in order to be accountable. In many institutions leaders are responsible for providing land and facilities.

But what else do leaders *owe?* What are artful leaders responsible for? Surely we need to include people. People are the heart and spirit of all that counts. Without people, there is no need for leaders. Leaders can decide to be primarily concerned with leaving assets to their institutional heirs or they can go beyond that and capitalize on the opportunity to leave a legacy, a legacy that

13

takes into account the more difficult, qualitative side of life, one which provides greater meaning, more challenge, and more joy in the lives of those whom leaders enable.

Besides owing assets to their institutions, leaders owe the people in those institutions certain things. Leaders need to be concerned with the institutional value system which, after all, leads to the principles and standards that guide the practices of the people in the institution. Leaders owe a clear statement of the values of the organization. These values should be broadly understood and agreed to and should shape our corporate and individual behavior. What is this value system based on? How is it expressed? How is it audited? These are not easy questions to deal with.

Leaders are also responsible for future leadership. They need to identify, develop, and nurture future leaders.

Leaders are responsible for such things as a sense of

quality in the institution, for whether or not the institution is open to influence and open to change. Effective leaders encourage contrary opinions, an important source of vitality. I am talking about how leaders can nurture the roots of an institution, about a sense of continuity, about institutional culture.

Leaders owe a covenant to the corporation or institution, which is, after all, a group of people. Leaders owe the organization a new reference point for what caring, purposeful, committed people can be in the institutional setting. Notice I did not say what people can do—what we can do is merely a consequence of what we can be. Corporations, like the people who compose them, are always in a state of becoming. Covenants bind people together and enable them to meet their corporate needs by meeting the needs of one another. We must do this in a way that is consonant with the world around us.

Leaders owe a certain maturity. Maturity as expressed

in a sense of self-worth, a sense of belonging, a sense of expectancy, a sense of responsibility, a sense of accountability, and a sense of equality.

Leaders owe the corporation rationality. Rationality gives reason and mutual understanding to programs and to relationships. It gives visible order. Excellence and commitment and competence are available to us only under the rubric of rationality. A rational environment values trust and human dignity and provides the opportunity for personal development and self-fulfillment in the attainment of the organization's goals.

Business literacy, understanding the economic basis of a corporation, is essential. Only a group of people who share a body of knowledge and continually learn together can stay vital and viable.

Leaders owe people space, space in the sense of freedom. Freedom in the sense of enabling our gifts to be exercised. We need to give each other the space to grow, to be ourselves, to exercise our diversity. We need to give each other space so that we may both *give* and *receive* such beautiful things as ideas, openness, dignity, joy, healing, and inclusion. And in giving each other the gift of space, we need also to offer the gifts of grace and beauty to which each of us is entitled.

Another way to think about what leaders owe is to ask this question: What is it without which this institution would not be what it is?

Leaders are obligated to provide and maintain momentum. Leadership comes with a lot of debts to the future. There are more immediate obligations as well. Momentum is one. Momentum in a vital company is palpable. It is not abstract or mysterious. It is the feeling among a group of people that their lives and work are intertwined and moving toward a recognizable and legitimate goal. It begins with competent leadership and a management team strongly dedicated to aggressive man-

17

agerial development and opportunities. This team's job is to provide an environment that allows momentum to gather.

Momentum comes from a clear vision of what the corporation ought to be, from a well-thought-out strategy to achieve that vision, and from carefully conceived and communicated directions and plans that enable everyone to participate and be publicly accountable in achieving those plans.

Momentum depends on a pertinent but flexible research and development program led by people with outstanding gifts and unique talents. Momentum results when a corporation has an aggressive, professional, inspired group of people in its marketing and sales units. Momentum results when the operations group serves its customers in such a way that the customer sees them as their best supplier of tools, equipment, and services. Underlying these complex activities is the essential role of the financial team. They provide the financial guidelines and the necessary ratios. They are responsible for equity among the various groups that compose the corporate family.

Leaders are responsible for effectiveness. Much has been written about effectiveness—some of the best of it by Peter Drucker. He has such a great ability to simplify concepts. One of the things he tells us is that efficiency is doing the thing right, but effectiveness is doing the right thing.

Leaders can delegate efficiency, but they must deal personally with effectiveness. Of course, the natural question is "how." We could fill many pages dealing with how to be effective, but I would like to touch on just two ways.

The first is the understanding that effectiveness comes about through enabling others to reach their potential—

19

both their personal potential and their corporate or institutional potential.

In some South Pacific cultures, a speaker holds a conch shell as a symbol of a temporary position of authority. Leaders must understand who holds the conch—that is, who should be listened to and when. This makes it possible for people to use their gifts to the fullest for the benefit of everyone.

Sometimes, to be sure, a leader must choose who is to speak. That is part of the risk of leadership. A leader must assess capability. A leader must be a judge of people. For leaders choose a person, not a position.

Another way to improve effectiveness is to encourage roving leadership. Roving leadership arises and expresses itself at varying times and in varying situations, according to the dictates of those situations. Roving leaders have the special gifts or the special strengths or the special temperament to lead in these special situations. They are acknowledged by others who are ready to follow them. (See "Roving Leadership.")

Leaders must take a role in developing, expressing, and defending civility and values. In a civilized institution or corporation, we see good manners, respect for persons, an understanding of "good goods," and an appreciation of the way in which we serve each other.

Civility has to do with identifying values as opposed to following fashions. Civility might be defined as an ability to distinguish between what is actually healthy and what merely appears to be living. A leader can tell the difference between living edges and dying ones.

To lose sight of the beauty of ideas and of hope and opportunity, and to frustrate the right to be needed, is to be at the dying edge.

To be a part of a throwaway mentality that discards goods and ideas, that discards principles and law, that discards persons and families, is to be at the dying edge.

21

To be at the leading edge of consumption, affluence, and instant gratification is to be at the dying edge.

To ignore the dignity of work and the elegance of simplicity, and the essential responsibility of serving each other, is to be at the dying edge.

Justice Oliver Wendell Holmes is reported to have said this about simplicity: "I would not give a fig for the simplicity this side of complexity, but I would give my life for the simplicity on the other side of complexity." To be at the living edge is to search out the "simplicity on the other side of complexity."

In a day when so much energy seems to be spent on maintenance and manuals, on bureaucracy and meaningless quantification, to be a leader is to enjoy the special privileges of complexity, of ambiguity, of diversity. But to be a leader means, especially, having the opportunity to make a meaningful difference in the lives of those who permit leaders to lead.

PARTICIPATIVE
PREMISES

What is it most of us really want from work? We would like to find the most effective, most productive, most rewarding way of working together. We would like to know that our work process uses all of the appropriate and pertinent resources: human, physical, financial. We would like a work process and relationships that meet our personal needs for belonging, for contributing, for meaningful work, for the opportunity to make a commitment, for the opportunity to grow and be at least reasonably in control of our own destinies. Finally we'd like someone to say "Thank you!"

Business has been moving for many years—and will

continue to do so—from a posture and a practice of management through power to a process of leadership through persuasion. This, of course, tends to make the use of formal organizational power out-of-date.

I believe that the most effective contemporary management process is participative management. Participative management is glibly discussed these days in a number of magazines and books, but it is not a theoretical position to be adopted after studying a few journals. It begins with a belief in the potential of people. Participative management without a belief in that potential and without convictions about the gifts people bring to organizations is a contradiction in terms.

Participative management arises out of the heart and out of a personal philosophy about people. It cannot be added to, or subtracted from, a corporate policy manual as though it were one more managerial tool.

Everyone has the right and the duty to influence decision making and to understand the results. Participative management guarantees that decisions will not be arbitrary, secret, or closed to questioning. Participative management is not democratic. Having a say differs from having a vote.

Effective influencing and understanding spring largely from healthy relationships among the members of the group. Leaders need to foster environments and work processes within which people can develop high-quality relationships—relationships with each other, relationships with the group with which we work, relationships with our clients and customers.

How does one approach the problem of turning the ideals about relationships into reality? There are no guaranteed formulas, but I would propose five steps as a starting point. Surely, you will revise and add to the list.

Respect people. This begins with an understanding of the diversity of their gifts. Understanding the diversity of these gifts enables us to begin taking the crucial step of trusting each other. It also enables us to begin to think in a new way about the strengths of others. Everyone comes with certain gifts—but not the same gifts. True participation and enlightened leadership allow these gifts to be expressed in different ways and at different times. For the CEO to vote on the kind of drill press to buy would be foolish. For the drill press operator (who should be voting on the kind of tool to use) to vote on whether to declare a stock split would be equally foolish.

Understand that what we believe precedes policy and practice. Here I am talking about both our corporate and personal value systems. It seems to me that our value system and world view should be as closely integrated into our work lives as they are integrated into our lives with our families, our churches, and our other activities and groups.

Many managers are concerned about their style. They

wonder whether they are perceived as open or autocratic or participative. As practice is to policy, so style is to belief. Style is merely a consequence of what we believe, of what is in our hearts.

Agree on the rights of work. Each of us, no matter what our rank in the hierarchy may be, has the same rights: to be needed, to be involved, to have a covenantal relationship, to understand the corporation, to affect our destiny, to be accountable, to appeal, to make a commitment. I will say more about the rights of work in the next chapter.

Understand the respective role and relationship of contractual agreements and covenants. Contractual relationships cover such things as expectations, objectives, compensation, working conditions, benefits, incentive opportunities, constraints, timetables, etc. These are all a part of our normal life and need to be there.

But more is needed—particularly today when the majority of us who work can properly be classified as volunteers. The best people working for organizations are like volunteers. Since they could probably find good jobs in any number of groups, they choose to work somewhere for reasons less tangible than salary or position. Volunteers do not need contracts, they need covenants.

Covenantal relationships enable corporations and institutions to be hospitable to the unusual person and to unusual ideas. Covenantal relationships enable participation to be practiced and inclusive groups to be formed. The differences between covenants and contracts appear in detail in "Intimacy."

Understand that relationships count more than structure. Every educational institution goes through periodic evaluation by some sort of accreditation committee. A small college with which I have been associated went through such an evaluation recently. The committee's report noted an especially high level of trust between the president, who was to retire soon, and the faculty. To create this trust with the next president, the committee recommended that the college make the necessary changes in its "structures." The president was justifiably amused. Structures do not have anything to do with trust. People build trust.

Finally, one question: Would you rather work as a part of an outstanding group or be a part of a group of outstanding individuals? This may be the key question in thinking about the premises behind participation.

THEORY
FASTBALL

The Polish government once announced that they were going to "initiate strict meat rationing in order to restore faith in socialism." The Iraqi government once sent envoys to twenty nations to explain their country's peaceful attitude "before and during the war." Obvious contradictions like these often spring from a shortsightedness, a preoccupation with one's own point of view. There is danger in considering a single point of view.

Unfortunately, the tantalizing subject of effectiveness and productivity has been too often considered only from one point of view—the manager's. We are obliged to look at this subject from the perspective of the one from whom management expects effectiveness and productivity. What is the producer's side of this question? We need to spell out a new concept of work.

Some people search for the key to productivity in money and "perks" and the complexity of materialism. Some lose themselves in politically dictated togetherness or in the many adversarial relationships with which we are so familiar.

For many of us who work, there exists an exasperating discontinuity between how we see ourselves as persons and how we see ourselves as workers. We need to eliminate that sense of discontinuity and to restore a sense of coherence in our lives.

Work should be and can be productive and rewarding, meaningful and maturing, enriching and fulfilling, healing and joyful. Work is one of our greatest privileges. Work can even be poetic.

One way to think about work is to ask how poets and

philosophers would lead corporations. At Herman Miller, our poets and philosophers have mostly been designers —George Nelson, Charles Eames, Robert Propst, Bill Stumpf. In every case, these very special people have made a significant contribution to Herman Miller. In every case, these people have been outstanding teachers.

George Nelson has helped me to see that the word "creativity" applies in the way that a physicist would talk about the process of discovery. The creative process in today's corporation is by its very nature difficult to handle. Anything truly creative results in change, and if there is one thing a well-run bureaucracy or institution or major corporation finds difficult to handle, it is change.

In almost every group nearly everybody at different times and in different ways plays two roles: One is creator, and the other is implementer. This key relationship is often underestimated and mistakenly cast in the light of "boss" and "subordinate." Hierarchy is inappropriate here. Oftentimes, implementing has to be as creative as the creative act to which it is responding. This is the point at which management and leadership find things most difficult in being open to the influence of others.

My wife's brother happens to be Jim Kaat. For twenty-five years, he was a great major-league pitcher. In the mid-sixties, he had the memorable opportunity of pitching against the famous Sandy Koufax in the World Series.

Once I asked Jim about Koufax's greatness. He explained that Koufax was unusually talented, was beautifully disciplined and trained. "In fact," he said, "Koufax was the only major-league pitcher whose fastball could be heard to hum. Opposing batters, instead of being noisily active in their dugout, would sit silently and listen for that fastball to hum. They would then take their turn at the plate already intimidated."

I told Jim how Koufax's opponents could have solved

this problem. It would have been a simple solution. I said, "You could have made me his catcher."

You see, every great pitcher needs an outstanding catcher. I am such an unskilled catcher that Koufax would have had to throw the ball more slowly to me, and we could have deprived him of his greatest weapon.

In baseball and business, the needs of the team are best met when we meet the needs of individual persons. By conceiving a vision and pursuing it together, we can solve our problems of effectiveness and productivity, and we may at the same time fundamentally alter the concept of work.

Any concept of work rises from an understanding of the relationship between pitchers and catchers. The following list of rights is for pitchers and catchers alike. These rights are essential if there is to be a new concept of work. It is not a complete list of rights, of course, but these eight are essential.

1. *The Right to be Needed.* Can I use my gifts? In the long run, this most effectively meets the group need. Our son Chuck was big for his age and, therefore, able to carry a trombone. The grade-school bandleader assigned him to that instrument because the band needed a trombonist and no one else was big enough. The band's need was legitimate. Unfortunately, Chuck had no desire at all to play the trombone. He gave it up shortly and the band lost its trombonist.

The right to be needed, of course, includes a meaningful personal relationship to the group's goals.

2. *The Right to Be Involved.* Involvement needs to be structured, and includes the privileges of problem ownership and risk. It has a minimum of three elements. While simple in theory, these are difficult to put in place.

We need a system of *input*—leaders must arrange for involvement on everybody's part.

We need a system of *response*—leaders must make that involvement genuine. A great error is to invite people to be involved and to contribute their ideas and then to exclude them from the evaluation, the decision-making process, and the implementation.

We need to take *action*—together we must translate our interaction into products and services on behalf of our customers.

This matter of involvement is not to be taken lightly. The process of involvement can cost dearly. The price is that leaders must be genuinely open to the influence of others.

3. The Right to a Covenantal Relationship. When I think about covenantal relationships, I think of them in relation to contractual relationships. Both exist. Both are commitments. Certainly, contractual relationships, whether written or understood, are normal in business and industry.

The contractual relationship tends to be legal and is based on reciprocity.

Covenantal relationships fill deep needs, enable work to have meaning and to be fulfilling. They make possible relationships that can manage conflict and change. (See "Intimacy.")

True covenants, however, are risky because they require us to be abandoned to the talents and skills of others, and therefore to be vulnerable. The same risks as one has when falling in love. If you wonder whether this whole idea has a place in corporate life, please ask your nearest poet or philosopher.

4. The Right to Understand. Together, we need to understand our *mission.* We have the right to understand the strategy and the direction of the group.

Everyone has the right to understand his or her *personal career path.* We all need to know the opportunities in this group and how we can realize them. Inherent in this is the right to enlarge one's competence through study and new experiences.

We need to understand our *competition.* At Herman Miller, we give a variety of annual awards for outstanding performance. One of the winners a few years ago, a man highly skilled in designing and building unique equipment and fixtures, decided to use part of his award to travel and see company installations. In the process of visiting a number of our sales offices, he also saw those of various competitors.

This was a new experience for him. He wished he had known the quality and closeness of our competition long ago because he could have worked more effectively.

We need to understand and be "at home" in our *working environment*—both the human environment and the physical environment. There needs to be a visible order and a "sense of place" so that we may know who we are and where we fit. Our environments should have a human scale, and we have a right to beauty.

We have the right to understand the elements of our *contract* covering compensation, working conditions, shared benefits, incentive opportunities, expectations, and normal constraints.

Essential to good understanding is that leaders clarify the responsibility of each member of the group. These and other elements of the right to understanding obligate leaders to communicate, to educate, and to evaluate.

5. The Right to Affect One's Own Destiny. Few elements in the work process are as important to personal dignity as the opportunity to influence one's own future. The processes of performance evaluation, promotion, and transfer should always take place with the person's involvement.

6. *The Right to Be Accountable.* To be accountable, we need to have the opportunity to contribute to the group's goals. We need the opportunity to share in the ownership of the group's problems and also the inherent risk. We need to have our contributions measured according to previously understood and accepted standards of performance, and this transaction needs to take place in an adult-to-adult relationship.

At the heart of being accountable is the matter of caring. In many areas of business, sadly, "to care" is an innovation.

7. *The Right to Appeal.* We need to build into our group structures a nonthreatening avenue of appeal. The purpose of this is to ensure against any arbitrary leadership that may threaten any of a person's rights we have been discussing. One of the most important responsibilities of leaders is to work hard at offering these rights to those we lead.

8. The Right to Make a Commitment. What exactly is the right to make a commitment? Recently, I was talking with a group of people in Boston whose company had been acquired by a larger company. More recently, their parent company had been acquired by a still larger company. I asked one of them how this process had affected his life. He said, "It makes me hedge my bets. I no longer can make a commitment. I no longer know who I am."

To make a commitment, any employee should be able to answer "yes" to the following question: Is this a place where they will let me do my best? How can leaders expect a commitment from the people they lead, if those people feel thwarted and hindered? And believe me, there are many obstacles constructed by unthinking leaders.

One of the key inhibitors to the right to commitment in corporations today occurs when, in the perception of those who follow, the leadership is not rational. One of the key responsibilities of leadership is the obligation to be rational.

These are some of my ground rules for working. If any one of us is to catch someone's fastball, there must be a mitt. The rights of work make a sort of mitt. Without them, even a catcher as good as Koufax's great partner Johnny Roseboro might drop the ball.

ROVING
LEADERSHIP

It was Easter Sunday morning and the large church was filled. The processional was ready to begin. The three pastors, the senior choir, two children's choirs poised at the back of the church—weeks of planning and preparation were about to be fulfilled.

As the organist struck the first chord, a middle-aged man in the center of the church began to sweat profusely, turned an ashen gray, rose partially out of his seat, stopped breathing, and toppled over onto his daughter sitting next to him.

And what did these pastors, organists, and choirs do? They did nothing.

But in less than three seconds, a young man with experience as a paramedic was at the stricken man's side. Quickly and expertly he opened the airway and restored breathing. After several minutes, making sure the sick man's condition was stabilized and on a signal from the paramedic, six men lifted him carefully and carried him quickly to the back of the church where he was laid on the floor to await the arrival of the ambulance, which, having been called for immediately by some unknown person, was already on its way.

When the man was laid on the floor near the waiting children's choir, two youngsters fainted. Two doctors from the congregation were immediately on the scene. One stepped in to help the young man care for the patient; the other immediately looked after the two children.

At this point a man thrust his head into the group gathered around the patient and said, "Are you going to want oxygen?" And when the doctor said, "Yes," he immediately handed it to him, having anticipated the need and gone to find the oxygen bottle.

While all these things were going on, the man's wife (who was in the senior choir and did not know what was happening—only that the service was being momentarily delayed) was sensitively informed and brought to her husband's side. Others quieted the children's choirs, reassured them that the man was going to be okay and that they should begin to compose themselves for the service. The paramedics arrived, put the man in the ambulance, and took him to the hospital.

As you can imagine, a tender and poignant service now began. At the end of the service, the pastor was able to announce that the man had suffered a severe allergic reaction; his condition was stable; the outlook was positive.

The point in telling you this story is to show that while

47

this church has a hierarchy of more than thirty appointed and elected professionals, committee members, board members, and others, the hierarchy did not respond swiftly or decisively. It is difficult for a hierarchy to allow "subordinates" to break custom and be leaders. The people who *did* respond swiftly and effectively are roving leaders. Roving leaders are those indispensable people in our lives who are there when we need them. Roving leaders take charge, in varying degrees, in a lot of companies every day.

More than simple initiative, roving leadership is a key element in the day-to-day expression of a participative process. Participation is the opportunity and responsibility to have a say in your job, to have influence over the management of organizational resources based on your own competence and your willingness to accept problem ownership. No one person is the "expert" at everything.

In many organizations there are two kinds of leaders—

both hierarchical leaders and roving leaders. In special situations, the hierarchical leader is obliged to identify the roving leader, then to support and follow him or her, and also to exhibit the grace that enables the roving leader to lead.

It's not easy to let someone else take the lead. To do this demands a special openness and the ability to recognize what is best for the organization and how best to respond to a given issue. Roving leadership is an issue-oriented idea. Roving leadership is the expression of the ability of hierarchical leaders to permit others to share ownership of problems—in effect, to take possession of a situation.

When roving leadership is practiced, it makes demands on each of us—whether we're a hierarchical leader, a roving leader, or a good follower. It's a demanding process. It demands that we be enablers of each other.

Roving leadership demands a great deal of trust and a

clear sense of our interdependence. Leadership is never handled carelessly—we share it, but we don't give it away. We need to be able to count on the other person's special competence. When we think about the people with whom we work, people on whom we depend, we can see that without each individual, we are not going to go very far as a group. By ourselves we suffer serious limitations. Together we can be something wonderful.

Roving leadership also demands discipline. Interestingly, though in organizations like ours we need a lot of freedom, there's no room for license. Discipline is what it takes to do the job.

It is not a matter primarily of whether or not we reach our particular goals. Life is more than just reaching our goals. As individuals and as a group we need to reach our potential. Nothing else is good enough. We must always be reaching toward our potential.

The condition of our hearts, the openness of our attitudes, the quality of our competence, the fidelity of our experience—these give vitality to the work experience and meaning to life. These are what it takes to make roving leadership possible. And roving leadership, freely and openly practiced together, is the vehicle we can use to reach our potential.

INTIMACY

Intimacy is at the heart of competence. It has to do with understanding, with believing, and with practice. It has to do with the relationship to one's work.

Everyone knows you can't run a good restaurant with absentee management. A young man I know went to eat lunch one day at his regular restaurant. It was unusually busy. He managed to get a menu, but before the waitress came to take his order his lunch hour had evaporated. Genuinely concerned that the owner should know what had happened, he mentioned it to the cashier in a friendly way and went back to work. That night, the owner of the restaurant arrived at the young man's house, unannounced, with dinner—enough dinner for two nights.

This kind of intimacy with one's work leads to solid competence.

Being an effective department supervisor on a manufacturing floor is fundamentally different from giving seminars about it.

In the same way, war games are different from battle. Those who have been there know the heightened sense of reality and unreality, and the odor of fear and risk and death. Only the heart-pounding experience of battle can bring that intimacy.

Those of you who have had real experience with machinery and equipment and even buildings know that they have personalities of their own. Intimacy with a job leads one to understand that when training people to do a job, one needs to teach not only the skill of the job but the art of it as well. And the art of it always has to do with the personality of both the operator and the machine. Intimacy is the experience of ownership. This often arises out of difficulty or questions or exasperation, or even survival.

Beliefs are connected to intimacy. Beliefs come before policies or standards or practices. Practice without belief is a forlorn existence. Managers who have no beliefs but only understand methodology and quantification are modern-day eunuchs. They can never engender competence or confidence. They can never be truly intimate.

Functionally and technologically we are concerned with intimacy. We should be concerned with intimacy when we design the organizational structures which, after all, are the road maps that help us to work together. Intimacy concerns us personally, professionally, and organizationally.

Intimacy with our work directly affects our accountability and results in personal authenticity in the work process. A key component of intimacy is passion.

You should not think that you can come to intimacy easily or by following a formula. Nor is intimacy easily preserved. It has its enemies. In our group activities, intimacy is betrayed by such things as politics, short-term measurements, arrogance, superficiality, and an orientation toward self rather than toward the good of the group.

Superficiality in a special way is an enemy of intimacy. When one thinks carefully about why certain people who are competent, well educated, energetic, and well supported with good tools fail, it is often the red thread of superficiality that does them in. They never get seriously and accountably involved in their own work.

Intimacy is betrayed by the inability of our leaders to focus and provide continuity and momentum. It is betrayed by finding complexity where simplicity ought to be. Leaders who encumber people rather than enabling them betray intimacy.

Intimacy has its champions too.

I was inspired by a Charles Kuralt segment reporting on a talented high school gymnast paralyzed from the waist down. The young athlete was really good, and it was fun to see how accomplished he had become. Something he said applies in a special way to each of us: "I don't come with the wheelchair. The wheelchair comes with me."

This is the way it is at work. We don't come with our companies—they come with us, because no company or institution can amount to anything without the people who make it what it is. Our companies can never be anything we do not want ourselves to be. When we look at work in that relationship to ourselves, we develop a real intimacy with work, an intimacy that adds value to work and to our organizations.

We find intimacy through a search for comfort with

ambiguity. We do not grow by knowing all of the answers, but rather by living with the questions.

Intimacy rises from translating personal and corporate values into daily work practices, from searching for knowledge and wisdom and justice. Above all, intimacy rises from, and gives rise to, strong relationships. Intimacy is one way of describing the relationship we all desire with work.

Charles Eames used to enjoy talking about "good goods." He was talking about good materials, good solutions, good products. This helped me to understand that the "good goods" of the art of leadership is the sacred nature of our relationships. Intimacy should be part of the relationships we build at work.

Broadly speaking, there are two types of relationships in industry. The first and most easily understood is the contractual relationship. The contractual relationship covers the quid pro quo of working together. I've mentioned this kind of relationship before. But more is needed, particularly today when the majority of workers are, essentially, volunteers.

Three of the key elements in the art of working together are how to deal with change, how to deal with conflict, and how to reach our potential. A legal contract almost always breaks down under the inevitable duress of conflict and change. A contract has nothing to do with reaching our potential.

Alexander Solzhenitsyn, speaking to the 1978 graduating class of Harvard College, said this about legalistic relationships: "A society based on the letter of the law and never reaching any higher, fails to take advantage of the full range of human possibilities. The letter of the law is too cold and formal to have a beneficial influence on society. Whenever the tissue of life is woven of legalistic relationships, this creates an atmosphere of spiritual mediocrity that paralyzes men's noblest impulses." And later: "After a certain level of the problem has been reached, legalistic thinking induces paralysis; it prevents one from seeing the scale and the meaning of events." *(A World Split Apart,* New York: Harper & Row, 1978, pp. 17–19, 39.)

Covenantal relationships, on the other hand, induce freedom, not paralysis. A covenantal relationship rests on shared commitment to ideas, to issues, to values, to goals, and to management processes. Words such as love, warmth, personal chemistry are certainly pertinent. Covenantal relationships are open to influence. They fill deep needs and they enable work to have meaning and to be fulfilling. Covenantal relationships reflect unity and grace and poise. They are an expression of the sacred nature of relationships.

Covenantal relationships enable corporations to be hospitable to the unusual person and unusual ideas. Covenantal relationships tolerate risk and forgive errors. I am convinced that the best management process for today's environment is participative management based on covenantal relationships. Look for the "good goods" of quality relationships that prevail in a corporation as you seek to serve.

How can we begin to build and nurture intimacy? Well, one way to begin is by asking questions and looking for answers. How does the company connect with its history? What business is it in? Who are the people and what are their relationships with one another? How does the company deal with change and conflict? Most important, perhaps, what is their vision of the future? Where are they going? What do they want to become?

Leaders are obliged to think about these questions. Both the act and the art of leadership, if we are to be intimate with our work, demand this.

From time to time I am asked, "What is your personal goal for Herman Miller?" When one loves jazz, one thinks of Louis Armstrong. When one truly enjoys baseball, one thinks of Sandy Koufax. When one appreciates stabiles, one thinks of Alexander Calder. When we respond to the French Impressionists, we think of Renoir. Each of these beautifully talented, beautifully trained, beautifully disciplined persons is special to us because he is a gift to the spirit.

My goal for Herman Miller is that when people both inside the company and outside the company look at all of us, not as a corporation but as a group of people working intimately within a covenantal relationship, they'll say, "Those folks are a gift to the spirit."

WHITHER CAPITALISM?

Who serves as a soldier at his own expense? Who plants a vineyard without eating any of its fruit? Who tends a flock without getting some of its milk? . . . For it is written in the law of Moses, "You shall not muzzle an ox when it is treading out the grain." Is it for oxen that God is concerned?

I CORINTHIANS, 9:7–9

In our effort to understand the capitalist system and its future, what should we keep in mind? We should begin with a concept of persons.

First, as a Christian I believe each person is made in the image of God. For those of us who have received the gift of leadership from the people we lead, this belief has enormous implications.

Second, God has given people a great diversity of gifts. Understanding the diversity of our gifts enables us to begin taking the crucial step of trusting each other. The simple act of recognizing diversity in corporate life helps us to appreciate and connect the great variety of gifts that people bring to the corporation.

Third, I believe that God, for reasons that we may not always understand, has provided us a population mix—a population mix for which leaders are held accountable.

This concept of persons within the capitalist system holds important implications for everybody—Christian or not. These implications lie primarily in the quality of our relationships. Relationships are at the heart and center of the capitalist system, both contractual relationships and deeper, more enabling covenantal relationships—two kinds of relationships discussed in the previous essay.

One of the great problems of the capitalist system during its first couple of hundred years is that it has been primarily an exclusive system. It has been built primarily around contractual relationships, and it has excluded too many people from both its process and a generally equitable distribution of results. The issue here is much more than financial reward: Most people never get the opportunity to be meaningfully involved in the working of the system.

I do not know of a better system, but the capitalist system can be improved, both in practice and in theory, with the influence of an inclusive perspective. The aim is not primarily to improve the results, although that is a significant possibility. The aim is to embody the concept of persons, for a substantial concept of persons must underlie an inclusive system. A belief that every person brings an offering to a group requires us to include as many people as possible. Including people, if we believe in the intrinsic value of their diversity, will be the only path open to us.

It may be that the capitalist system cannot survive as an exclusive arrangement. In our social structures today we're under tremendous pressure, particularly from advertisers, to believe that we have an endless appetite for

65

anything as long as it breathes an air of exclusiveness. Behind all of this lurks the idea of getting it for yourself! Take care of yourself! When one sits back quietly and thinks about it, these attitudes are, in fact, simply the implementation of selfishness. Exclusiveness breeds selfishness.

When God said we are made in his image, he placed no other qualification on that concept. So we are driven to see both the appropriateness of our diversity and the beauty and two-way nature of our interdependence. Therefore we reject exclusivity. We covet inclusiveness.

How can we begin to make capitalism an inclusive process? Well, there are a number of ways. First of all, by acknowledging both a Christian and a humanistic concept of people. Each of us is needed. Each of us has a gift to bring. Each of us is a social being and our institutions are social units. Each of us has a deep-seated desire to contribute.

An inclusive system requires us to be insiders. We are interdependent, really unable to be productive by ourselves. Interdependency requires lavish communications. Lavish communications and an exclusive process are contradictory.

One can define this inclusive approach in three ways. First, there are always certain marks of being included:

- being needed
- being involved
- being cared about as an individual
- fair wages and benefits
- having the opportunity to do one's best (Only leaders willing to take risks can give this opportunity.)
- having the opportunity to understand
- having a piece of the action—productivity gains, profit sharing, ownership appreciation, seniority bonus

Second, the inclusive approach makes me think of a corporation or business or institution as a place of fulfilled

67

potential. For me it helps to think about the concept of a place of fulfilled potential by thinking about some gifts that leaders owe. Leadership is a condition of indebtedness. Leaders who have an inclusive attitude think of themselves as owing, at the very least, the following:

- space: a gift to be what I can be
- the opportunity to serve
- the gift of challenge: we don't grow unless we're tested (constraints, like facts, are enabling friends)
- the gift of meaning: not superfluous, but worthy; not superficial, but integral; not disposable, but permanent

Here are a couple of views about leadership and inclusiveness. I think it's fairly obvious which one I endorse.

At an American Management Association conference for presidents, an invited speaker in all seriousness said, "I want men that are vicious, grasping, and lusting for power." He also gave us his version of the Golden Rule— "He who has the gold makes the rules."

On the other hand, some time ago at a board of directors meeting I attended, Bill Stumpf, an industrial designer, then teaching at the University of Wisconsin, posed the following questions:

- Should a corporation challenge life?
- Does the artist have a role in the corporation?
- What is the relationship of expectation to performance?
- What warrants corporate existence?

Finally, here is a third way to understand and define an inclusive approach. Inclusive capitalism requires something from everyone. People must respond actively to inclusiveness. Naturally, there is a cost to belonging.

- Being faithful is more important than being successful. If we are successful in the world's eyes but unfaithful in terms of what we believe, then we fail in our efforts at insidership.

- Corporations can and should have a redemptive purpose. We need to weigh the pragmatic in the clarifying light of the moral. We must understand that reaching our potential is more important than reaching our goals.

69

- We need to become vulnerable to each other. We owe each other the chance to reach our potential.

- Belonging requires us to be willing and ready to risk. Risk is like change; it's not a choice.

- Belonging requires intimacy. Being an insider is not a spectator sport. It means adding value. It means being fully and personally accountable. It means forgoing superficiality.

- Last, we need to be learners together. The steady process of becoming goes on in most of us throughout our lifetime. We need to be searching for maturity, openness, and sensitivity.

When people fulfill these requirements, bear the cost, then the opportunities to be needed, to be involved, and to participate become rights.

The only way to keep these rights is to exercise them constructively, intelligently, cooperatively, and productively. Really including other people means helping them understand. It means giving others the chance to do their best. Being included, according to the diversity of our gifts, is fundamental to the equity that justice requires and inspires.

If one accepts the premises concerning the concept of persons, if one accepts the idea of covenantal relationships, if one seeks to practice the inclusive approach in the capitalist system, will it work? In the capitalist system there are standards of performance to be met, ratios to be maintained, service to be given, profits to be made, the future to be assured, jobs to be secured.

Can this approach work? I do not know for sure, but there are many encouraging signals and perhaps preliminary results. There are also real difficulties. This approach to management is not easy. It is very demanding and it can at times be discouraging because, after all, we are all human. Inclusiveness means including normal human problems in the system.

I am certainly aware of the growing sophistication of trained managers these days. They are a large part of the capitalist system. Their skills at quantification are admirable. But I sometimes wonder how often they focus on the

71

spirit? Do they examine what will be important tomorrow and not just the operational matters of today?

Though necessary and desirable, it is easy to include people procedurally in committees, lunches, or even in profits, just as it is easy to write contracts.

It is more difficult, but far more important, to be committed to a corporate concept of persons, the diversity of human gifts, covenantal relationships, lavish communications, including everyone, and believing that leadership is a condition of indebtedness.

Even with this commitment, we should hope that our efforts at opening doors into the capitalistic system are never described in the words of an older Israeli who was quoted in *National Geographic*. She said, speaking of the younger Zionists: "They opened up the doors of the world, but they closed up the heavens forever." *(National Geographic,* 168, no. 1 (July 1985): pp. 4–5.)

72

GIANT TALES

What is a giant? Well, giants are many things. People like you and me may become giants.

Giants see opportunity where others see trouble. One of the giants in Herman Miller's history was a man named Jim Eppinger. Jim was the sales manager of the company through the thirties and forties and, in particular, during our transition from making good-quality, traditional copies of furniture to learning how to sell the revolutionary new designs of Rhode and Nelson and Eames. Those were tough years, really tough years that only a few people still understand.

Once I sat in on a luncheon with my father and Jim

Eppinger—these two old cronies who had made the company survive during the Depression. They were talking, with a sense of humor and nostalgia, about some of the difficulties of the early days and, in particular, the Depression.

My father recalled for Jimmy a time they had been together at Jim's home in New Jersey during Christmastime and mentioned how much he was aware that Jim's family had no Christmas tree nor any gifts. Dad knew it was because the company did not have enough money to pay the sales commissions that were due.

Dad mentioned that Jim probably didn't remember that time, but it was very real to my father, because he felt it was his fault that Jim's family would have no Christmas. But Jim said, "I remember that evening as if it were yesterday, because for Marian and me it was one of the highlights of our lives." And my dad, surprised, said, "How could that possibly be?" Jim said, "Well, don't you remember? That was the night you gave me the New York territory. It was the greatest opportunity I've ever had."

Giants give others the gift of space, space in both the personal and the corporate sense, space to be what one can be. One of my favorite giants is George Nelson. In the late 1940s Herman Miller introduced George's marvelous and, to this day, appropriate line of residential furniture. During the weeks when these designs were being readied for introduction to the market, another giant appeared on the scene in an exhibit at the Museum of Modern Art: Charles Eames.

George worked very hard to persuade both my father and Jim Eppinger to write Charles and arrange to add Charles's designs to the Herman Miller program. My father said something like this to George: "We're just getting ready to introduce your first products to the market. We're not a large company. We'll never pay very much in royalties. Do you really want to share this small opportu-

75

nity with another designer?" George's response was something like this: "Charles Eames is an unusual talent. He is very different from me. The company needs us both. I want very much to have Charles Eames share in whatever potential there is."

In the ensuing years, Charles Eames became recognized as the greatest furniture designer since Chippendale.

Giants catch fastballs. One of the giants at Herman Miller is a man named Pep Nagelkirk, who is probably the most talented model maker I have ever heard of. He has served Herman Miller designers for thirty-five years. He has a special gift for translating ideas and sketches into prototypes. He is an indispensable part of every design program we launch. He is a fastball catcher.

Now a fastball may be enough for a pitcher, but it is never enough for a team. Corporations and people can throw good ideas around as often as they want. Without giant catchers like Pep Nagelkirk, those ideas may eventually disappear. We have hundreds of giant catchers like Pep Nagelkirk at Herman Miller. Without giant catchers there can be no giant pitchers.

Giants have special gifts. Another of our giants is a man named Howard Redder, a department supervisor who retired some time ago. Howard never went to high school. He worked in the factory all of his adult life and worked his way up the ladder and became one of the best department supervisors we ever had. But beyond that, Howard has a special gift.

He is the most sensitive and most effective enabler of handicapped employees the company has had. This is important, because, as a company, we strongly believe that the diversity of the population must be reflected in our company's population. That special ability, to give a handicapped person the space and support and encouragement to be productive and to honor the sense of

77

involvement that all of us have, makes another kind of giant.

Giants enable others to express their own gifts. The last giant I'd like to mention is my father. During the Depression days, when he and a few others were dealing with the company's day-to-day survival, he was able to accept people like Gilbert Rhode, and later George Nelson, Charles Eames, and Alexander Girard at a time in his life when he knew practically nothing about design, designers, or the design process. But he had the great insight to see the diversity of their gifts, which in turn enabled him to be personally and corporately abandoned to the exercise of their gifts.

There are at least two things we learn about corporations from these tales of giants. The first is that while productivity is important, giving space to giants is much more important. The second is that giving space to giants lets them and others practice the "roving leadership" I discussed earlier. These two lessons may, from time to time, be hard on the hierarchical leadership. But if you want a corporation to be truly effective, you will need to help corporations be open to giants at all levels.

TRIBAL
STORYTELLING

Dr. Carl Frost, a good friend and adviser to our company, tells a story of his experience in Nigeria during the late sixties.

Electricity had just been brought into the village where he and his family were living. Each family got a single light in its hut. A real sign of progress. The trouble was that at night, though they had nothing to read and many of them did not know how to read, the families would sit in their huts in awe of this wonderful symbol of technology.

The light-bulb watching began to replace the customary nighttime gatherings by the tribal fire, where the tribal storytellers, the elders, would pass along the history of the tribe. The tribe was losing its history in the light of a few electric bulbs.

This story helps to illustrate the difference between scientific management and tribal leadership. Every family, every college, every corporation, every institution needs tribal storytellers. The penalty for failing to listen is to lose one's history, one's historical context, one's binding values. Like the Nigerian tribe, without the continuity brought by custom, any group of people will begin to forget who they are.

Herman Miller's stock of values is an example of the continuity I'm talking about. Herman Miller is a group of people who, working together and, more often than we care to admit, fighting together, have made a difference. This has made us a leading company. Our stock of values has risen from our history and our customs. These values are concrete examples of what a vital company today passes along through tribal storytelling. Perhaps you and your company share some of these values with us.

We are a research-driven product company. We are not a market-driven company. It means that we intend, through the honest examination of our environment and our work and our problems, to meet the unmet needs of our users with problem-solving design and development. Thus, we are committed to good design in products and systems.

We are committed to extending that design into the work environment, including especially our own architecture and facilities that serve us and our customers. We are committed to applying the same standard of design to all of our communications and graphics. We are committed to good design even in the design of situations, especially in those situations and events that bear on the quality of our relationships with each other.

We intend to make a contribution to society. We wish to make that contribution through the products and services we offer, and through the manner in which we offer them. In an era of high technology, we wish to be a "high-touch" company that makes the environmental connection between persons and technology in the markets we choose to serve. We intend to be socially responsible and responsive.

As Tom Pratt, a friend and member of my work team at Herman Miller, has observed, "Life and work are intrinsically meaningful and, therefore, worthy of enlightened attention and support."

We are dedicated to quality. Quality, as D.J., my father, has said, is a matter of truth. When we talk about quality, we are talking about quality of product and service. But we are also talking about the quality of our relationships and the quality of our communications and the quality of our promises to each other. And so, it is reasonable to think about quality in terms of truth and integrity.

My dictionary, when defining the word integrity, recommends looking up the word honor. Among many choices, there is the phrase: "A fine sense of one's obligations." This, I believe, is the way to look at quality.

We must become, for all who are involved, a place of realized potential. This is a value at Herman Miller. Any organization, meaning the people who constitute such a body, needs to offer outstanding education and training. We each have the right, at Herman Miller, within the participative process, to genuine opportunity.

Each of us, but especially those with the responsibility for leadership, must be dedicated to making the "gift of space" available to others—that is, space to be what we can be in the corporate environment.

We each have the right to this gift of space without regard to color, creed, sex, or level of talent and coordination. In our goal to be a place of realized potential, the Herman Miller population must be a reflection of God's diversity, not of our choices.

We are committed to a high sense of initiative in doing everything we can to make capitalism an inclusive system of relationships, not an exclusive structure of barriers.

We are committed to using responsibly our environment and our finite resources. We are devoted to outstanding performance through our stewardship of talent and resources, of tools and jigs, of ideas and designs, of facilities and situations. All combine to provide a legitimate *result in equity* for employee owners, customers, investors, the public, and the communities in which we live and work.

We commit voluntarily our energy and talent, as well as our financial resources, to those agencies and institutions whose purpose is the common good. We cannot live our lives isolated from the needs of society.

It is essential to us that we preserve our future economically. Profit, like breathing, is indispensable. While it is not the sole goal of our lives, in the context of our opportunities, profit must be a result of our contribution.

We at Herman Miller acknowledge that issues of the heart and spirit matter to each of us. They matter in our families, in our work, and in our extracurricular activities. We are emotional creatures, trying through the vehicles of product and knowledge and information and relationships to have an effect for good on one another both personally and through what we can do to improve the environment.

In a difficult and fractured and complex world, in problems of failure and of success, but especially in the joys and tragedies of our personal lives, we touch each other. This "touching" is at the heart of who we are.

Deep in who we are today lies waiting a challenge. It is not an external mystery—the question of what we can be lies within us, for whatever we do expresses the character of the people who are this company.

We are deeply committed to the Scanlon idea, a plan for practicing participative management, including productivity and profit sharing, used by quite a few companies in the United States. There are some beautiful and fundamental reasons why this way of participative management especially thrives at Herman Miller.

It enables the expression of the diverse gifts of persons with an emphasis on creativity and on the quality of the process. It fuels the generation of ideas, the solving of problems, and the managing of change and conflict. While we have worked at it for over thirty-five years, it's still an idea, an idea with tremendous impounded energy. It is the constant search for what is and what can be that enables persons and groups to reach their potential.

In a group like Herman Miller, we have both personal diversity and corporate diversity. When we think of *cor-*

porate diversity, we think about the gifts and talents and commitment that each of us as individuals bring to the group effort. Channeled correctly and integrated properly, our diversity can be our greatest strength. But there is always the temptation to use these gifts for our personal benefit rather than dedicating them to the best interest of the group. If used selfishly, they will cause serious internal erosion. The process of integration is simply abandoning oneself to the strengths of others, being vulnerable to what others can do better than we can.

The concept of human equality is not affected by the corporate hierarchy. We understand that the corporation is an entity only in that it is an expression of each of us as individuals. We know that the soul and spirit, the gifts, the heart and dignity of each of us combine to give the corporation these same qualities. We who invest our lives in Herman Miller are neither the grist of a corporate mill nor the hired guns of distant, mysterious stockholders. As a faculty and staff are a university, so we are Herman Miller. The corporation can never be something we are not.

To a great extent we at Herman Miller, a very diverse group of individuals, share this set of common values. The roots of this value system differ almost person by person, but our spoken and understood expressions of it are remarkably coherent.

Shared ideals, shared ideas, shared goals, shared respect, a sense of integrity, a sense of quality, a sense of advocacy, a sense of caring—these are the basis of Herman Miller's covenant and value system. Our system of values may not be generic. It must be explicit. The system and the covenant around it make it possible for us to work together, not perfectly to be sure, but nevertheless in a way that enables us to have the potential to be a gift to the spirit.

We work to maintain these values. Yet a system of

beliefs is always threatened by change, and change is something no one can avoid. Successful entrepreneurships tend to become corporations. Successful corporations tend to become institutions. Institutions foster bureaucracy, the most superficial and fatuous of all relationships. Bureaucracy can level our gifts and our competence. Tribal storytellers, the tribe's elders, must insistently work at the process of corporate renewal. They must preserve and revitalize the values of the tribe. They nourish a scrutiny of corporate values that eradicates bureaucracy and sustains the individual. Constant renewal also readies us for the inevitable crises of corporate life.

The goal of renewal is to be a corporate entity that gives us space to reach our potential as individuals and, through that, as a corporation. Renewal comes through genuine service to others. It cannot come about through a process of mere self-perpetuation. Renewal is an outward orientation of service, rather than an inward orientation of maintenance. Renewal is the concern of everyone, but it is the special province of the tribal storyteller.

Every company has tribal stories. Though there may be only a few tribal storytellers, it's everyone's job to see that things as unimportant as manuals and light bulbs don't replace them.

WHO OWNS
THIS PLACE?

Broadly speaking, there are three categories of owners in the typical American corporation. The first group, those normally thought of as owners, invest mere cash in the business. The second, because they have dedicated their working years to the corporation, invest their lives and their gifts in the corporation. The third group, essential contributors to the corporation, invest some special skill or talent or creative energy and have a strong commitment to the corporation, but part-time.

To understand a corporation, we must understand the characteristics of its owners as expressed through their management and through their personal behavior. If anyone is to serve the corporation, either as a professional consultant or as a full-time employee and owner, that person must understand the attitudes of ownership.

What should be our attitude of ownership? Are the owners committed to short-term or long-term performance? Physical growth or maturity? To what kind of management process is the ownership committed? Do they think of work as an illness or an opportunity? In the sense of ideas and special talents, do they see their role as stewards or possessors? In the sense of the complex environment in which we all work and live, are the owners dedicated to serving people or to accumulating money and things? In other words, is mere material accumulation and measurement what life is all about for the owners?

One perception of ownership appeared in a recent business magazine, when the president of a privately owned company was asked if his tactics would be different if he were running a public company. His response was "If I knew my compensation next year would be based on this year's return on equity, hell no, I wouldn't act the same. You've only got a few years at the top in a public company to make your killing. You want to put every penny on the bottom line to wind up with the juiciest retirement package you can get."

One sees an admirable counterpoint in a thoughtful book, *Servant Leadership* by Robert Greenleaf, an executive with AT&T for twenty years. "Love is an undefinable term, and its manifestations are both subtle and infinite." It has only one "absolute condition: unlimited liability! As soon as one's liability for another is qualified to any degree, love is diminished by that much." *(Servant Leadership,* New York: Paulist Press, 1977, p. 38.)

Owners are liable for hard assets and also a legacy for their corporate heirs. At Herman Miller, owners and corporate heirs are often the same people, as are owners and employees. This began to happen more than twenty years ago when stock was sold to a small group of executives who were making a career commitment to the company.

Today we are one of the few public companies in the United States where 100 percent of the full-time regular employees in the U.S. who have completed one year of service are stockholders. These two roles bring responsibilities and rewards.

A story I once heard illustrates this idea. A friend of mine used to teach in Harlem. He thought it might be a good idea to take these city kids out to the country for a week at camp. One of the first things he did, not unnaturally, was to organize a baseball game.

A curious thing happened. Nobody would play in the outfield. He soon discovered the reason for this: The outfield was surrounded by the woods where all sorts of unknown dangers lay. My friend assigned two kids to each outfield position. One would hold the glove; one would watch the woods. Each person and each duty was essential. And the game went on.

At Herman Miller, there is an owner and an employee in *every* position. Because everybody acts sometimes as employee and sometimes as owner and sometimes as a little of both, employee-stockholders complement the participative management process which we have had since 1950. The Scanlon Plan, introduced under the leadership of Dr. Carl F. Frost, is in a very real sense the paradigm of employee ownership.

Employee stock ownership is essential to a declaration of identity. Motivation is not a significant problem: Herman Miller employees bring that with them by the bushel. But people need to be liberated, to be involved, to be accountable, and to reach for their potential. We believe that more and more working owners are winning the struggle for identity and meaning against anonymity and frustration.

Employee stock ownership is also clearly a competitive reality. Nothing is being given. Ownership is earned and paid for. The heart of it is profit sharing, and there is no sharing if there are no profits. Risk and reward are connected logically and fairly.

There is no smug condescension at play here. Rather, there is a certain morality in connecting shared accountability as employees with shared ownership. This lends a rightness and a permanence to the relationship of each of us to our work and to each other.

Stock ownership is a marvelous vehicle for involving an entire family in the career of those of us who work for corporations. There is a compelling coherence to reasons for employee ownership.

There are also some clear implications. There is risk personally and there is risk corporately. While it's great to work for gains, one also has to be ready for the losses.

Recently an employee and owner at Herman Miller, a

woman working on her master's degree at Aquinas College, told me how a couple of her instructors who work at other companies asked, "What is the bottom line on the Scanlon Plan?" I suggested that she call their attention to the first section of that year's annual report, interviews conducted, edited, and printed without either review or approval on my part. Some companies might find this kind of risk unbearable, but it is a kind of risk taken constantly by employee-owners in a good participative process. More often than not, the results more than justify the risk.

Another implication is that everybody must live up to some important expectations. In the position of owners, we become more accountable for our personal performance. Owners cannot walk away from concerns. So, the accountability of all of us begins to change.

Ownership demands increasing maturity on everyone's part. Maturity is probably expressed best in a continually rising level of literacy: business literacy, participative literacy, ownership literacy, competitive literacy. The group of owners committed to the same organization, to the same goals, to the same value systems must be knowledgeable in many areas. Ownership demands a commitment to be as informed about the whole as one can be.

In the end, it is important to remember that we cannot become what we need to be by remaining what we are. At Herman Miller we are committed to doing everything we can to grow both as employees and owners. As those two roles merge, adversarial postures—labor versus management or supplier versus producer or retailer versus consumer—will begin to disappear. The merging of employees and owners is already happening in many places.

The capitalist system cannot avoid being better off by having more employees who act as if they own the place.

COMMUNICATE!

In most vital organizations, there is a common bond of interdependence, mutual interest, interlocking contributions, and simple joy. Part of the art of leadership is to see that this common bond is maintained and strengthened, a task certainly requiring good communication. Just as any relationship requires honest and open communication to stay healthy, so the relationships within corporations improve when information is shared accurately and freely.

The best way to communicate the basis of a corporation's or institution's common bonds and values is through behavior. Communication through behavior happens all the time. With large organizations spread out all over the world, we must have additional ways to

101

communicate besides behavior, especially to communicate intangible and crucial and fragile information to widespread groups of people.

What *is* good communication? What does it accomplish? It is a prerequisite for teaching and learning. It is the way people can bridge the gaps formed by a growing company, stay in touch, build trust, ask for help, monitor performance, and share their vision. Communication clarifies the vision of participative ownership as a way of building relationships within and without the corporation.

Good communication is not simply sending and receiving. Nor is good communication simply a mechanical exchange of data. No matter how good the communication, if no one listens all is lost. The best communication *forces* you to listen.

At the root, communication and one of its forms, language, are commitments to a convention, a culture. Dishonest or careless communication tells us as much about the people involved as it does about anything else. Communication is an ethical question. Good communication means a respect for individuals.

The real challenge is to make good communication a handy and well-used tool. Then you are likely to pick it up and use it without thinking.

Our grandson once locked himself in the bathroom. Despite his mother's best efforts to get the door open, she failed. She called in the police, who also failed to open the door. (All the while, our grandson kept reaching under the door to touch his mother's hand. Talk about good communication!) Finally his mother called the fire department. By the time the fire trucks arrived, there was quite a scene on the front lawn. The firemen promptly broke down the door with their axes, tools they certainly know how to use.

When our son Chuck arrived, at the height of the suspense, he could not quite figure out what was happening.

There was no fire or smoke, but his bathroom door and its frame were in shambles.

At the office the next day, he was complaining to a colleague about the damage. The colleague observed that there might be a management lesson in the story. "A fireman has two tools, an axe and a hose. If you call him, you're going to get one."

Everybody is more likely to use familiar and trusted tools. Among a leader's most trusted and familiar tools are communication skills. Whether or not we use them well is another question, and like the fireman's axe, skillful communication comes with obligations.

A number of obligations go along with good communication. We must understand that access to pertinent information is essential to getting a job done. The right to know is basic. Moreover, it is better to err on the side of sharing too much information than risk leaving someone in the dark. Information is power, but it is pointless power if hoarded. Power must be shared for an organization or a relationship to work.

Everyone has a right to, and an obligation for, simplicity and clarity in communication. We owe each other truth and courtesy, though truth is sometimes a real constraint, and courtesy inconvenient. But make no mistake —these are the qualities that allow communication to educate and liberate us.

We are obligated to practice the art of scrutiny. The art of scrutiny has to do with several things: a respect for the English language, an acknowledgment that muddy language usually means muddy thinking and that our audience may need something special from us. The art of scrutiny will uncover what I call "third-class mail," missives without meaning. Junk mail serves no more purpose in the corporate setting than it does in our homes.

If we think of good communication as a tool and remember these obligations, we can avail ourselves of a way to expand our work and our lives. Tools do something. And so does communication. Communication performs two functions, described by two "action-prone" words: educate and liberate.

"Educate" comes from two Latin words that mean "lead" or "draw out." Good communication draws out of us an awareness of the meaning of working together. We cannot do good research and development, we cannot make decisions, we cannot get orders—we simply cannot *do business* without learning what we expect from each other.

Teaching and learning underlie business literacy and action. Business literacy is the "why" of what corporations do, and the action is the "what" they do.

How else does communication educate us? Good communication can educate us to the realities of our economy and the need for our performance within that economy. Only through good communication can we learn the needs and demands of our customers.

Only through good communication can we convey and preserve a common corporate vision. Communication can sharpen, embody, and help enact that vision. We all understand that in our family and corporate lives the *absence* of comment and question and response and opinion is a powerful communication. These are just a few examples of how good communication can educate us.

Good communication liberates us to do our jobs better. It is as simple as that. Good corporate communication allows us to respond to the demands placed on us and to carry out our responsibilities. This really means, too, that leaders can use communication to free the people they lead. To liberate people, communication must be based on logic, compassion, and sound reasoning.

This rationality extends to the system of words and signs that a company and its customers adopt together.

Good, lucid communication means commitment to the same symbols of good work and success. Plato said that a society cultivates whatever is honored there. Let us make no mistake about what we honor. If these symbols are understood, we can and do enable each other.

As a culture or a corporation grows older and more complex, the communications naturally and inevitably become more sophisticated and crucial. An increasingly large part that communication plays in expanding cultures is to pass along values to new members and reaffirm those values to old hands.

A corporation's values are its life's blood. Without effective communication, actively practiced, without the art of scrutiny, those values will disappear in a sea of trivial memos and impertinent reports.

There may be no single thing more important in our efforts to achieve meaningful work and fulfilling relationships than to learn and practice the art of communication.

PINK ICE
IN THE URINAL

Every year in April, at the time of the Masters Golf Tournament in Augusta, the state of Georgia hosts about forty national and international industrial leaders for a one-week tour of the state. The purpose of the tour is to entice industry to move to Georgia. Two or three days at the Masters is an effective way to encourage participation in the tour.

Over the years the tour has been effective. Georgia has an outstanding record of bringing new industry to the state. Since Herman Miller has a plant in Roswell, just northeast of Atlanta, one year we were invited to be one of the host industries.

Naturally, we formed a committee to make plans for this event. In the discussion of the committee, one well-meaning person suggested that one way to dress up the facility was to put pink ice in the urinals. Despite the good intentions behind this idea, I take pink ice as a signal. Would pink ice in the urinals *really* help attract more industry to Georgia?

Some months ago, I was on what is known in the financial industry as a "dog and pony show." Our team was in Boston, making a presentation to some sophisticated financial analysts. After the presentation and during the question-and-answer period, one of the analysts said to me, "What is one of the most difficult things that you personally need to work on?" He seemed very surprised when I said, "The interception of entropy."

I am using the word "entropy" in a loose way, because technically it has to do with the second law of thermodynamics. From a corporate management point of view, I

110

choose to define it as meaning that everything has a tendency to deteriorate. One of the important things leaders need to learn is to recognize the signals of impending deterioration.

I have made a list of these signals over the years. As you read this list, remember that many people in large organizations relish apathy. They often fail to see the signs of entropy:

- a tendency toward superficiality
- a dark tension among key people
- no longer having time for celebration and ritual
- a growing feeling that rewards and goals are the same thing
- when people stop telling tribal stories or cannot understand them
- a recurring effort by some to convince others that business is, after all, quite simple (The acceptance of complexity and ambiguity and the ability to deal with them constructively are essential.)
- when people begin to have different understandings of words like "responsibility" or "service" or "trust"
- when problem-makers outnumber problem-solvers

- when folks confuse heroes and celebrities

- leaders who seek to control rather than liberate

- when the pressures of day-to-day operations push aside our concern for vision and risk (I think you know that vision and risk can never be separated.)

- an orientation toward the dry rules of business school rather than a value orientation that takes into account such things as contribution, spirit, excellence, beauty, and joy

- when people speak of customers as impositions on their time rather than as opportunities to serve

- manuals

- a growing urge to quantify both history and one's thoughts about the future (You may be familiar with people who take a look at a prototype and say, "In 1990 we'll sell $6,493,000 worth"—nothing is more devastating because then you plan either to make that happen or to avoid it.)

- the urge to establish ratios

- leaders who rely on structures instead of people

- a loss of confidence in judgment, experience, and wisdom

- a loss of grace and style and civility

- a loss of respect for the English language

If you and your corporation are committed to being as good as you can be, beware of pink ice in the urinals.

WHAT'S NEXT?

At times in business, the congruence of principles and practice—or their incongruence—comes sharply into focus. Reviewing performance is a time like that, a time to ask what we are trying to do, evaluate how we are doing, and then ask "What's next?"

Performance reviews, done well, are a good way of re-examining goals, realigning principles and practices, and gauging progress. Everyone should do this. Reviewing performance should be done in a timely way, with the direct involvement of the person whose performance is being reviewed. Both the people and the process should be directed toward reaching human potential.

For jobs easily described and work easily measured, there are good procedures to follow in corporations and institutions. But many jobs, especially those entailing responsibility for leadership of the corporation or institution, are not black-and-white, cannot be measured easily, and must be examined over long periods of time.

Leaders, in a special way, are liable for what happens in the future, rather than what is happening day to day. This liability is difficult to measure, and thus the performance of leaders is difficult to measure. Though we do need to review past results and processes, the emphasis on the duties and performance of leaders has to be on the future. It is especially hard to remember that today's performance from a leader succeeds or fails only in the months or years to come. Much of a leader's performance cannot be reviewed until *after* the fact.

Today's trust enables the future. We also enable the

future by forgiving the mistakes we all make while growing up. We free each other to perform in the future through the medium of trust.

I recently led a discussion group of about fifteen people at Herman Miller. We had introduced a "just in time" inventory-management program. One of the women in the group asked if I understood and was committed to this program. My answer was that I did not understand it completely but was committed to its success. This gave her pause. She was trying to figure out a tactful way of asking me how that could possibly be true.

When I asked her what her job was, she said that she worked in the engineering department. "How are things going there?" I asked. "Just fine," she said. I asked her if I should be comfortable about what was going on in the engineering department, and she told me that, by and large, I could be.

Then I asked if she was comfortable about the way I

115

was doing my job. She told me that she was. Catching the drift of the conversation, she added quickly that she did not understand everything I did. It was quite easy for the two of us, under the watchful eyes of the group, to agree that it was not necessary for us to understand completely what the other did or was accountable for. We could, nevertheless, be wholeheartedly committed to each other's role and each other's success.

As the group talked this idea over, we realized that, while understanding is an essential part of organized activity, it just is not possible for everybody to know everything and understand everything. The following *is* essential: We must trust one another to be accountable for our own assignments. When that kind of trust is present, it is a beautifully liberating thing.

Even trust will not make the nature of the future more certain. But the uncertain nature of the future does not necessarily make leadership a hazardous occupation.

Many of the things in this book might be discussed in a thoughtful and effective way when linked with corporate strategy. Philosophy can, and should, be put into practice.

An effective CEO will review the performance of the senior management team. As part of a covenantal relationship, every leader must review the performance of the people he or she leads, and no doubt there are many ways of doing this. Usually I send members of my management team a list of requests and questions ahead of time. Anything else they wish to bring to the review is fine with me. Our agreement is always "no holds barred."

Here are some requests I have made to each senior manager before the performance review.

- Please prepare a brief review, one or two pages, of how you feel you have done in comparison to your annual plan. What is the most important achievement in your area?

117

- Please prepare a one-page or shorter statement of your personal management philosophy. Describe your personal plans for continuing education and development for the coming year.

- Please think about ways for us to approach our accountability (with many others) for the future of the corporation, and our joint accountability for your future career in the corporation. What kind of changes will be required by the growth picture we are plotting?

- Review your thoughts on team building at the senior management team level, commenting perhaps on parity in responsibility, in accountability, in compensation, and as part of our succession plan. What ideas do you have for things we should reflect on at future senior management retreats?

- Prepare to discuss your thoughts on our competition and where we need to respond to it and what our response should be. Perhaps the following can trigger your thinking: Who is creeping up on us? How do various competitors beat us out? In product, service, selling capability, marketing and advertising, dealer distribution, or pricing?

- Please describe for me what you think your role at Herman Miller can be as one of the "corporate storytellers" who play an active role in the transmission of the corporate culture. What do you think this corporate culture is?

- How can I personally have more time to focus on such things as strategy, our value system, participation, continuity, and team building?

- Please identify five key projects and/or goals you have as a key leader at Herman Miller and in which you feel I can be of help or support.

Simply asking questions is another important part of performance reviews. Asking the *right* questions is a knack that needs working on. Here are a few questions I have asked my senior managers to consider.

- Would you be willing to share your philosophy of management with your work team?
- What are a few of the things that you expect most and need most from the CEO?
- What do you want to do (to be)? What are you planning to do about it?
- Who are you? How do you see yourself personally, professionally, and organizationally?
- Does Herman Miller need you?
- Do you need Herman Miller?
- What are you doing to realize the potential of our Scanlon Plan philosophically, functionally, educationally, and in the management of relationships?
- If you were "in my shoes," what one key area or matter would you focus on?
- What significant areas are there in the company where you feel you can make a contribution but feel you cannot get a hearing?
- What have you abandoned?

- Do you have any feelings of failure in any particular area?

- What two things should we do to work toward being a great company?

- What should grace enable us to be?

- What will you do in the coming year to develop your three highest-potential persons (and who are they)?

- In the past year, what, from the perspective of integrity, most affected you personally, professionally, and organizationally?

- What are three signals of impending entropy you see at Herman Miller? What are you doing about it?

- What are three examples of budding synergy in your area and how we can capitalize on them?

Finally, I think there is value in considering thoughts from other leaders, leaders not necessarily in the same area as one's own. Mahatma Gandhi once wrote that there were seven sins in the world: wealth without work; pleasure without conscience; knowledge without character; commerce without morality; science without humanity; worship without sacrifice; politics without principle. Performance considered in light of those seven sins would be a well-reviewed performance indeed.

SOME THOUGHTS FOR CEOS WHO BUILD BUILDINGS

How does one transform verbal and often abstract statements into steel and stone? We are all familiar with how the Greeks and the Romans left the marks of their culture in architecture. The Mayans, too, expressed their culture in distinctive buildings. Broadly, you might say that architecture deals with the relationship of people and the environment. As a company, Herman Miller deals with that relationship every day.

In thinking about facilities and their relation to corporate cultures, I consulted my dictionary about the word "culture." From a number of choices, most of which had to do with biology, I selected this statement: "A particular state or stage of civilization." To me this definition links rather nicely to the idea of a corporate culture, but leaves me with a question: How should we think about man-made facilities as a state or stage of civilization?

You can frequently be helped in efforts to understand a problem by asking yourself questions. Here are a few about physical places and social places. These questions lead me to think about the working environment in a variety of ways:

- Does what I do count?
- Does what I do make a difference to anybody?
- Why should I come here?
- Can I be somebody here?
- Is there *for me* any rhyme or reason here?
- Can I "own" this place?
- Do I have any rights?
- Does coming here add any richness to my life?
- Is this a place where I can learn something?

- Would I show this place to my family—or am I ashamed to show it to them—or does it just not matter?
- Is there anybody here I can trust?
- Is this place open to my influence?
- Does it help to understand architecture as a societal response?

The physical environment matters a great deal, but it is not as important as the management environment. The physical environment is likely to be a consequence of certain elements of the management environment. In that sense the facility will reflect the context of a corporation, its leadership, and its values.

During a time of financial strain in the economy and in the company, an employee-owner at Herman Miller asked why we had spent so much money on three ponds surrounding our main site in Zeeland, Michigan. In short, this person was asking how these ponds reflected our company and its values, a question he had every right to ask.

Buildings do not exist in a vacuum, and neither did these ponds. The ponds exist to gather runoff created by the roofs of our buildings, to keep our neighbors' land from flooding, and to satisfy local land use laws. They furnish a ready supply of water in case of fire. They form a beautiful addition to our site. We even have a company picnic around them.

These ponds, only a small part of Herman Miller's facilities, reflect our company's attitudes about business, our community, and our people. All facilities should make this kind of sense in their contexts. In turn, facilities should create a context for a state or stage of corporate civilization.

Facilities can aspire to certain qualities as an expression of a civilization. Some of these qualities are readily apparent. Some are not.

A facility should be a place that people can possess. Taking possession of the facility in which we work is closely linked to the idea of ownership. There is a fundamental difference, after all, between owners and renters. It is fair to say that renters are no-fault owners.

Facilities should enable and empower people to do their best. Facilities, like managers, should be vulnerable. They should encourage a rising level of knowledge about corporate life: literacy about business, the competition, relationships, and ownership. Our facilities must encourage lavish communications.

A facility should be a place of realized potential. It should be a "high touch" place. A place where we connect persons to each other and to technology in an effective and human way.

Now, having said all of these things, some philosophical and some practical, about facilities and the corporate culture, is there a way to be specific? Of course there is. We should make it our goal to create an environment that

- encourages an open community and fortuitous encounter
- welcomes all
- is kind to the user
- changes with grace
- is person-scaled
- is subservient to human activity
- forgives mistakes in planning
- enables this community (in the sense that an environment can) to reach continually toward its potential
- is a contribution to the landscape as an aesthetic and human value
- meets the needs we can perceive
- is open to surprise
- is comfortable with conflict
- has flexibility, is nonprecious and nonmonumental

It is important that we be prudent stewards of corporate assets and at the same time avoid savings at the cost of good long-range planning and a quality environment.

It is important that we keep future options open. This will demand real discipline because there is always a great drive to pin everything down if possible.

It is important that everyone understand the context in which our facilities function and the context and value they create for us.

It is important that we avoid an overcommitment or rigidity to a single function or need. Experience has shown us that we need varying utilization patterns open to us and that we need open-ended growth possibilities. One of our goals is to build *the indeterminate building.*

Another goal is to ask the right questions about facilities. Perhaps Bucky Fuller did that best.

Buckminster Fuller, the philosopher, inventor, and designer (I have never quite known exactly what to call Bucky!) was touring a new building that an excellent architect, Norman Foster, had just completed in the English countryside. Norman had carefully prepared for the visit and had asked his staff to anticipate every question Bucky could possibly pose. As Norman and Bucky approached the building, which looked as if it could have been a huge

127

extrusion landed in the meadow by a giant helicopter, Norman reviewed in his mind all the answers, all the angles.

Bucky went along silently as they moved through the impressive building. At last he turned and pierced Norman with his steady, twinkling gaze and asked simply, "How much does it weigh?"

TO MAKE ONE
VICE PRESIDENT,
MIX WELL . . .

The art of leadership dwells a good deal in the future, in providing for the future of the organization, in planting and growing other leaders who will look to the future beyond their own. These future leaders, at some point in their careers, receive the title of vice president. They are important to the daily operations of a corporation or an institution, but their future is vital to the future of the group. Picking vice presidents with all these conditions in mind is not easy.

A few years ago, faced with the task of choosing several new vice presidents, I composed a memo to my senior management team. The decisions to be made in the process of choosing vice presidents are significant both for the people involved and for the organization. We are not only setting the tone and direction concerning management and leadership competence, we are dealing very specifically with the legacy we will leave.

With that in mind, I suggested three groups of thoughts that had to be dealt with in meeting this important challenge.

First, the corporation requires several things from leaders in making this decision. The corporation requires

- that the position be clearly one with responsibility and accountability on the officer level
- that the establishment of this officership be a signal to the organization of the significance of this responsibility and of its importance to the future of the corporation
- that the person who fills this position demonstrate not only personal performance and achievement but also the potential for continuing growth and accountability
- that this appointment be more a matter of expectancy and challenge than of reward, personally, professionally, organizationally

- that we interpret thoroughly to the organization each appointment

Second, the organization requires several things from the people chosen to be candidates for future leaders. These people must bring to their responsibilities certain characteristics, traits that should be present in all leaders, traits talked about in this book. A future leader

- has consistent and dependable integrity
- cherishes heterogeneity and diversity
- searches out competence
- is open to contrary opinion
- communicates easily at all levels
- understands the concept of equity and consistently advocates it
- leads through serving
- is vulnerable to the skills and talents of others
- is intimate with the organization and its work
- is able to see the broad picture (beyond his own area of focus)
- is a spokesperson and diplomat

- can be a tribal storyteller (an important way of transmitting our corporate culture)
- tells *why* rather than *how*

Third, beyond being a spokesperson in our organization, the new vice president should share in the basis for our values. He or she should be able to advocate Herman Miller's unique character to the world at large and within the corporation. The candidate should understand and speak for

- the corporate value system
- good design (in all its facets)
- participative management
- the human and ethical expression of the character of this corporation

Since sending the memo, several of the people I work with have suggested some further ideas to consider in the situation of choosing vice presidents. These additions come from a variety of experience and, as one of the people put it, "from having been burned." Here are their observations.

- The only kind of leadership worth following is based on vision.

- Personal character must be uppermost.

- If we are going to ask a person to lead, can we determine ahead of time whether he or she has gaps between belief and practice, between work and family?

- When talking about leadership, one always ends up talking about the future, about leaving a legacy, about followers. In other words, leadership intertwines the most important aspects of an organization: its people and its future. We need, therefore, to proceed very slowly and carefully.

- When choosing officers, provide for possible failure and a graceful withdrawal. Promotion to officership should be decided in a group, with no slim majority. The process should include complete commitment and no reservations. After all, the way we move managers around, you may inherit a work team that you cannot, or will not want to lead.

- What does the company physician say about the candidate?

- What do the person's peers have to say?

133

- Would you seek out this person as a key resource on an important task force?

These are important additions. Choosing leaders is the most vital and important matter corporations and institutions face. What characteristics of a good leader will you add?

WHY SHOULD
I WEEP?

Do grown men weep? Sure. Should grown men weep? Of course. Anyone in touch with reality in this world knows there are lots of reasons to weep. We weep over triumphs and over tragedies. Most good people weep over admirable actions and deplorable ones.

Some people might say "Why should Max weep? He's the Chairman and CEO. What problems could he possibly have?" Well, my joys and sadnesses may not be the same as everyone else's, but that does not make them any less real, believe me. Let me tell you about a good reason I had recently for weeping.

Our officers and director-level managers, sixty or seventy people, get together quarterly to review results, discuss plans, examine ideas and directions.

Shortly before one of these meetings, I had received a wonderful letter from the mother of one of our handicapped employees. It was a touching letter of gratitude for the efforts of many people at Herman Miller to make life meaningful and rich for a person who is seriously disadvantaged. Because we have a strong, albeit a quiet, effort going on in the company to empower the disadvantaged and to recognize the authenticity of everyone in the group, it seemed to be a good idea to read this letter to the officers and directors.

I almost got through this letter but could not finish. There I stood in front of this group of people—some of them pretty hard-driving—tongue-tied and embarrassed, unable to continue. At that point, one of our senior vice presidents, Joe Schwartz—urbane, elegant, mature—

strode up the center aisle, put his arm around my shoulder, kissed me on the cheek, and adjourned the meeting.

That is the kind of weeping we need more of. There is, unfortunately, another kind of weeping. Some years ago, one of our very competent managers left our headquarters to oversee a major installation in a large city. We wanted to give him all the help we could. One of our senior people asked him what he needed. The manager replied, "Tell the people at headquarters, when I call, to answer the phone and not to treat me like a customer."

Well, that's enough to make one weep.

There are, I suspect, many people who don't weep. Why? These people are not intimate with their work. They must not be trying to live up to their potential. They must think they cannot fail. They have no covenant with their group.

There are people who weep tears different from the two kinds I have talked about. There are tears of frustration and chagrin. That kind of weeping we can do without.

What *do* we weep over? What *should* we weep over? By now, having read this far you could probably predict that I would make a list. Here are some things we probably ought to weep about:

- superficiality
- a lack of dignity
- injustice, the flaw that prevents equity
- great news!
- tenderness
- a word of thanks
- separation
- arrogance
- betrayal of ideas, of principles, of quality
- jargon, because it confuses rather than clarifies
- looking at customers as interruptions
- leaders who watch bottom lines without watching behavior
- the inability of folks to tell the difference between heroes and celebrities

- confusing pleasure with meaning
- leaders who never say "Thank you"
- having to work in a job where you are not free to do your best
- good people trying to follow leaders who depend on politics and hierarchy rather than on trust and competence
- people who are gifts to the spirit

It would be easy to add some of the things under entropy in "Pink Ice in the Urinal." What would you add? Why should you weep?

THE MARKS OF
ELEGANCE

A few years ago, my wife and I and another couple were on a vacation in England and Scotland. One evening we were driving along a coastal road on our way to a small village and a pub supper. We were riding along a body of water but were not sure whether it was the English Channel or the Falmouth Estuary, where the Spanish Armada met its demise. We were debating this in the car when just ahead we saw two women and a child walking along the sidewalk. I said to my friend, "John, pull over there and I'll ask those ladies if this is the English Channel." So he did, and I rolled down the window and said, "Excuse me, ma'am, is that the English Channel?" She looked briefly over her shoulder and said, "Well, that's *part* of it."

Most of the time, when we consider ourselves and others, we are looking at only parts of people. The measure of individuals—and so of corporations—is the extent to which we struggle to complete ourselves, the energy we devote to living up to our potential. An elegant company frees its members to be their best. Elegant leaders free the people they lead to do the same.

Unfortunately, as in the example of my imprecise use of language, we often mistake a part for the whole. In business, sadly, this is often the case. There are great pressures to take a part for the whole, both in human terms and in financial ones.

At the office or in the plant, we see only sides of people. But as my father discovered about the millwright, a person mentioned in the first chapter, the parts of people we see at work may give us little idea of their completeness.

Likewise, a short-term look at the financial status of a

corporation or a dependence on immediate financial results will lead to a partial and perhaps twisted view of the
whole picture. A crucial element may be missing. We
may not be running the entire race. A friend of mine
described a colleague as great at running the "ninety-five-
yard dash." That is a distinction I can do without. Lacking
the last five yards makes the first ninety-five pointless.

Once again, I found myself brought up short by someone who pointed out to me that I had only part of the
picture. Curt Shosten, a panel assembler at Herman Miller, heard me tell the story of the "ninety-five-yard dash"
and wrote to complete the thought. He explained that
serious runners think of it as a *110-yard* dash so that no
one will beat you in the last few yards. That completes
this idea nicely. Think beyond the whole.

Parts are often mistaken for wholes. Ideas are viewed
as complete when they are incomplete. Relationships are
considered well formed when they are insufficiently

formed. Values are taken for final statements when, in fact, they are only beginnings. Were these parts recognized for what they are, and were we to work toward their completion—were we to keep "becoming" as individuals—we would be better off as persons, as corporations, and as institutions.

Elegant leaders always reach for completeness. What are some of the marks of elegance? What should leaders be searching for in their efforts to liberate people of high potential? The following ideas are some of the things that one needs to understand to be an elegant leader.

Contracts are a small part of relationships. A complete relationship needs a covenant.

Intelligence and education can ascertain the facts. Wisdom can discover the truth. The life of a corporation needs both.

To give one's time doesn't always mean giving one's involvement.

Hierarchy and equality are not mutually exclusive. Hierarchy provides connections. Equality makes hierarchy responsive and responsible.

Without forgiveness, there can be no real freedom to act within a group.

Opportunity must always be connected to accountability. This is not something hopelessly idealistic. Without the promise of accountability, there are no true opportunities and risks. Without true opportunity and risk, there is no chance to seize accountability; it will remain elsewhere.

A whale is as unique as a cactus. But don't ask a whale to survive Death Valley. We all have special gifts. Where we use them and how determines whether we actually complete something.

Goals and rewards are only parts, different parts, of human activity. When rewards become our goals, we are only pursuing part of our work. Goals are to be pursued.

In healthy and rational relationships, rewards complete the process by bringing joy. Joy is an essential ingredient of leadership. Leaders are obligated to provide it.

These are my marks of elegance. In a way, writing this book is my way of working toward completion, of trying to be the best that I can. What I hope, of course, is that some of the thinking in this book helps you to be what you can be.

By now, I hope we have created a kind of relationship in writing and reading this book together. I hope some of my remarks have sparked some comment from you and that you have read and written a lot between the lines. Our search for elegance, for completeness, for our potential is a search that should not end. What a marvelous horizon!

POSTSCRIPT

My introduction ended with a story about some columns that were too long. I want to end my book with a story about some columns that were too short—intentionally.

The noted English architect Sir Christopher Wren once built a structure in London. His employers claimed that a certain span Wren planned was too wide, that he would need another row of columns for support. Sir Christopher, after some discussion, acquiesced. He added the row of columns, but he left a space between the unnecessary columns and the beams above.

The worthies of London could not see this space from the ground. To this day, the beam has not sagged. The

147

columns still stand firm, supporting nothing but Wren's conviction.

Leadership is much more an art, a belief, a condition of the heart, than a set of things to do. The visible signs of artful leadership are expressed, ultimately, in its practice.